THE LITTLE BOOK OF
SUPERMUM

Copyright © Headline Publishing Group Limited 2026

The right of Stella Caldwell to be identified as the Author of the Work has been asserted by her in accordance with the Copyright, Designs and Patents Act 1988.

First published in 2026 by OH
An Imprint of HEADLINE PUBLISHING GROUP LIMITED

1

Disclaimer:

All trademarks, copyright, quotations, company names, registered names, products, characters, logos and catchphrases used or cited in this book are the property of their respective owners.

Apart from any use permitted under UK copyright law, this publication may only be reproduced, stored, or transmitted, in any form, or by any means, with prior permission in writing of the publishers or, in the case of reprographic production, in accordance with the terms of licences issued by the Copyright Licensing Agency.

Cataloguing in Publication Data is available from the British Library

ISBN 978-1-03543-685-9

Compiled and written by: Stella Caldwell
Editorial: Phoebe Hills
Designed and typeset in Avenir by: Tony Seddon
Project manager: Russell Porter
Production: Rachel Burgess
Printed and bound in Dubai

Headline's policy is to use papers that are natural, renewable and recyclable products and made from wood grown in well-managed forests and other controlled sources. The logging and manufacturing processes are expected to conform to the environmental regulations of the country of origin.

HEADLINE PUBLISHING GROUP LIMITED
An Hachette UK Company
Carmelite House, 50 Victoria Embankment, London EC4Y 0DZ

The authorised representative in the EEA is Hachette Ireland, 8 Castlecourt Centre, Dublin 15, D15 XTP3, Ireland (email: info@hbgi.ie)

www.headline.co.uk   www.hachette.co.uk

THE LITTLE BOOK OF

SUPERHERO WORDS
FOR MUMS WHO SAVE THE DAY

CONTENTS

INTRODUCTION - 6

8

CHAPTER
ONE

THE POWER OF MUM

44

CHAPTER
TWO

LOVE UNMATCHED

76

CHAPTER
THREE

MULTI-TASKER, MAGICIAN, MIRACLE WORKER...

104

CHAPTER
FOUR

ACROSS PLACE AND TIME

136

CHAPTER
FIVE

RAISING SUPERHEROES

166

CHAPTER
SIX

DEAR MUM...

INTRODUCTION

The word "mother" is one of the oldest in the world. Versions of it appear in nearly every culture, echoing across centuries and continents - and it's often the very first word we speak. Mum is the first person we run to, the voice that stays with us long after we've "grown up" and the one who somehow finds anything - even the missing sock we were sure didn't exist.

Fierce protectors, gentle comforters, tireless champions and unsung miracle workers — mums are all of these and more. This little book is a celebration of everything that makes them amazing. Within these pages, you'll discover a collection of quotes that span cultures and centuries - words from poets, presidents, comedians and everyday voices - that capture the magic of Mum. You'll also find fun facts and curious stats, from how many hours a mum spend on unpaid labour each year to how often she hears "Muuum!" before breakfast. And we'll dive into pop culture along the way, with mum-themed songs, film moments and literary gems that honour the heart and humour of motherhood.

Whether she's multitasking with mythical skill, healing broken hearts (or grazed knees) or quietly pulling strings behind the scenes, there's no denying the extraordinary power of Mum. But this isn't just sentimentality – expect laughs, surprises, maybe a few tears, and more than a few "that is so true" moments.

Whether you *are* a mum or simply love a mum, this book is for you. It's a tribute, a thank-you, a wink and a hug all rolled into one. So, curl up with a cuppa (if you ever get the chance), take a deep breath and enjoy this delightful little reminder of just how super mums really are.

The Power of Mum

Mums are like superheroes - minus the cape (usually). They're fierce, loving and somehow manage to keep everything running, even when life throws curveballs.

This chapter celebrates that unstoppable mum energy - the secret sauce that keeps families thriving and hearts full.

THE POWER OF MUM

> **A mother is a mother still,**
>
> **The holiest thing alive.**

Samuel Taylor Coleridge
English poet (1772–1834)

> **"**
> I am sure that if the mothers of various nations could meet, there would be no more wars.
> **"**

E. M. Forster
English novelist (1879–1970)

THE POWER OF MUM

> 66
> A mother is the truest friend we have, when trials heavy and sudden fall upon us...
> 99

Washington Irving
American short story writer, essayist and historian (1783–1859)

> **Perhaps it takes courage to raise children.**

John Steinbeck
American writer (1902–68)

"Mother" is one of the oldest words, with versions found in nearly every language.

This shared thread highlights just how deep and universal the role of a mother is. And of course, it's also one of the first words babies learn – a reflection of that special bond from the very start.

Let's hop around the globe and hear how "Mum" is said in different languages – a small word that carries a lot of meaning!

1. Spanish - *Mamá*
2. French - *Maman*
3. German - *Mama*
4. Italian - *Mamma*
5. Japanese - お母さん (Okaasan)
6. Russian - *Мама* (Mama)
7. Hindi - माँ (Maa)
8. Arabic — أم (Umm)

THE POWER OF MUM

> **The influence of a mother in the lives of her children is beyond calculation.**

James E. Faust
American religious leader (1920–2007)

> **A mother is the one who fills your heart in the first place.**

Amy Tan
American author (b.1952)

THE POWER OF MUM

> The mother is everything – she is our consolation in sorrow, our hope in misery and our strength in weakness.

Kahlil Gibran
Lebanese-American writer and poet (1883–1931)

> A mother's love is peace.
> It need not be acquired, it
> need not be deserved.

Erich Fromm
German-American psychologist and
psychoanalyst (1900–80)

THE POWER OF MUM

Part 1:
You know you're a SuperMum when...

1. You can find a missing sock faster than a detective.

2. You have a PhD in Negotiation (aka convincing kids to eat veggies).

3. You can juggle a washing machine, a microwave and a baby bouncer – all at the same time.

4. You know the *exact* sound of your child's "I'm not tired" voice at 10pm.

5. You have endless SuperMum patience (well, sometimes).

> Sleep is overrated when you're busy raising the future.

Anon

THE POWER OF MUM

> **"**
> My mother had a great deal of trouble with me, but I think she enjoyed it.
> **"**

Mark Twain
American writer (1835–1910)

> **There was never a great man who had not a great mother.**

Olive Schreiner
South African writer (1855–1920)

THE POWER OF MUM

SuperMum Affirmations

Being a mum means juggling countless roles with love and strength. The following affirmations will remind you of your incredible power and resilience – you're doing great!

1. I am doing my best, and that's enough.
2. I am strong, capable and resilient.

3. My love nourishes my children and family every day.

4. I deserve rest and self-care without guilt.

5. I am patient and present in every moment with my children.

6. I am proud of the balance I create between my needs and my family's.

7. I handle challenges with grace and confidence.

8. I am an incredible role model for my children.

THE POWER OF MUM

> When God thought of mother,
> He must have laughed
> with satisfaction,
> and framed it quickly – so rich,
> so deep, so divine,
> so full of soul, power and beauty
> was the conception.

Henry Ward Beecher
American minister (1813–87)

> Your love was like moonlight
> turning harsh things to beauty,
> so that little wry souls
> reflecting each other obliquely
> as in cracked mirrors...
> beheld in your luminous spirit
> their own reflection
> transfigured as in a shining stream,
> and loved you for what they are not.

Lola Ridge
Irish-American poet (1873–1941)

THE POWER OF MUM

> Without a mother, one cannot love. Without a mother, one cannot die.

Hermann Hesse
German-Swiss poet and novelist (1877–1962)

> A mother is she who can take the place of all others, but whose place no one else can take.

Gaspard Mermillod
Swiss Cardinal (1824–92)

> A suburban mother's role is to deliver children obstetrically once, and by car forever after.

Peter De Vries
American novelist (1910–93)

> Having children is like living in a frat house. Nobody sleeps, everything's broken and there's a lot of throwing up.

Ray Romano
American stand-up comedian and actor (b.1957)

THE POWER OF MUM

> **A mother is not a person to lean on, but a person to make leaning unnecessary.**

Dorothy Canfield Fisher
American author and social reformer (1879–1958)

> My doctor told me I would never walk again. My mother told me I would. I believed my mother.

Wilma Rudolph
American Olympic athlete (1940–94)

THE POWER OF MUM

The phrase "mother of all" (as in "the mother of all headaches" - sound familiar?) is used to describe something as the biggest, most powerful or most important of its kind (basically, the "SuperMum" of whatever you're talking about!).

The expression comes from Arabic and entered the English language through news media covering the Middle East.

> **"**
> It's not easy being a mom. If it were easy, fathers would do it.
> **"**

Betty White
American actress and comedian (1922–2021)

> We have a secret in our culture, and it's not that birth is painful. It's that women are strong.

Laura Stavoe
American educator and writer

> I always say, 'If you aren't yelling at your kids, you're not spending enough time with them.'

Reese Witherspoon
American actress and film producer (b.1976)

THE POWER OF MUM

Part 1:
Mums in the Movies

Terms of Endearment (1983)
A heartwarming story of a complex mother-daughter relationship over several decades.

Mother (***Madeo***, South Korea, 2009)
A gripping psychological thriller about a devoted mother determined to clear her mentally challenged son of murder charges.

Lady Bird (2017)
A coming-of-age dramedy about a fiercely independent teenager and her strong-willed mother.

Stepmom (1998)
A terminally ill mother struggles with accepting her children's future stepmother.

All About My Mother (*Todo sobre mi madre*, Spain, 1999)
After a tragedy, a mother searches for her son's father.

Imitation of Life (1959)
Two mothers – one Black, one white – navigate motherhood, race and ambition in 1950s America.

Tully (2018)
Follows a mum of three who forms an unexpected bond with her night nanny.

Fences (2016)
Viola Davis won an Oscar for her role as a strong and devoted mother holding her family together.

THE POWER OF MUM

> **❝**
> Insanity is hereditary; you get it from your children.
> **❞**

Sam Levenson
American humorist and TV host (1911–80)

> There were times, in middle school and junior high, I didn't have a lot of friends. But my mom was always my friend. Always.

Taylor Swift
American singer-songwriter (b.1989)

THE POWER OF MUM

The oldest verified first-time mother is Rajo Devi Lohan from India.

In 2008, at the age of 70, she gave birth to a baby girl following IVF treatment.

> But kids don't stay with you if you do it right. It's the one job where, the better you are, the more surely you won't be needed in the long run.

Barbara Kingsolver
American novelist and poet (b.1955)

Love Unmatched

Big, boundless and totally unconditional – there's nothing quite like a mum's love.

From the first embrace to the steady comfort through life's storms, this chapter celebrates the amazing one-of-a-kind love that only mums can give.

LOVE UNMATCHED

> **"**
> My mother was the most beautiful woman I ever saw. All I am I owe to my mother. I attribute my success in life to the moral, intellectual and physical education I received from her.
> **"**

George Washington
Founding Father and the first
US president (1732–99)

> A mother's arms are made of tenderness and children sleep soundly in them.

Victor Hugo
French author and poet (1802–85)

LOVE UNMATCHED

> **The love of a mother is the veil of a softer light between the heart and the heavenly Father.**

Samuel Taylor Coleridge
English poet (1772–1834)

> **"**
> No man is poor who has a Godly mother.
> **"**

Abraham Lincoln
Sixteenth US president (1809–65)

LOVE UNMATCHED

Mums develop what's often called "baby radar" - meaning that within days of birth, they can identify their baby's cry among others.

In a 2013 study, 22 out of 27 mothers (more than 80 per cent) correctly recognized their newborn's cry, just three to eight days postpartum.

> Paradise lies at the feet of your mother.

Islamic proverb

LOVE UNMATCHED

> But there's a story behind everything. How a picture got on a wall. How a scar got on your face. Sometimes the stories are simple, and sometimes they are hard and heartbreaking. But behind all your stories is always your mother's story, because hers is where yours begin.

Mitch Albom
American author and talk show host (b.1958)

> Mothers and their children are in a category all their own. There's no bond so strong in the entire world. No love so instantaneous and forgiving.

Gail Tsukiyama
American novelist (b. 1957)

LOVE UNMATCHED

> A mother's love is everything... It is what brings a child into this world. It is what moulds their entire being. When a mother sees her child in danger, she is literally capable of anything. Mothers have lifted cars off of their children and destroyed entire dynasties. A mother's love is the strongest energy known to man.

Jamie McGuire
American novelist (b.1978)

> No one in your life will ever love you as your mother does. There is no love as pure, unconditional and strong as a mother's love. And I will never be loved that way again.

Hope Edelman
American author and essayist (b.1964)

LOVE UNMATCHED

Part 2:
You know you're a SuperMum when...

1. You've perfected the art of ninja nappy changes in the dark.

2. You can pack a school lunch with one hand while making breakfast with the other.

3. You're fluent in toddler, tantrum and teenage eye-roll.

4. You've mastered the five-second rule for dropped snacks like a pro.

5. A two-minute coffee break feels as exciting as a spa day.

> Mum: The only job where you work 24/7 and get paid in hugs.

Anon

LOVE UNMATCHED

A mother's love for her child is like nothing else in the world. It knows no law, no pity. It dares all things and crushes down remorselessly all that stands in its path.

Agatha Christie
English author (1890–1976)

> My mom smiled at me. Her smile kind of hugged me.

R.J. Palacio
American author (b.1963)

LOVE UNMATCHED

From the moment they're born, newborns can recognize and respond to their mother's unique scent. This familiar smell provides a powerful sense of comfort and safety, helping to soothe a fussy or crying baby almost instantly.

Scientists believe a mother's scent can lower a baby's stress levels and plays a key role in forming strong emotional connections early in life.

> My mother's love has always been a sustaining force for our family, and one of my greatest joys is seeing her integrity, her compassion, her intelligence reflected in my daughters.

Michelle Obama
Attorney and former First Lady of the United States (b.1964)

LOVE UNMATCHED

> We are born of love;
> Love is our mother.

Rumi
Sufi mystic and poet (thirteenth century)

> **A mother's love liberates.**

Maya Angelou
American writer, poet and civil rights activist (1928–2014)

LOVE UNMATCHED

> **Whatever else is unsure in this stinking dunghill of a world, a mother's love is not.**

James Joyce
Irish novelist and poet (1882–1941)

> **The only love that I really believe in is a mother's love for her children.**

Karl Lagerfeld
German fashion designer and photographer (1933–2019)

Mum brain: Powered by love, distracted by everything else.

Anon

> **Behind every great kid is a mum who's pretty sure she's winging it.**
>
> **Anon**

LOVE UNMATCHED

> my mother
> is pure radiance.
>
> she is the sun
> i can touch
> and kiss
>
> and hold
> without
> getting burnt.

Sanober Khan
Indian author and poet

> No one in the world can take the place of your mother. Right or wrong, from her viewpoint you are always right. She may scold you for little things, but never for the big ones.

Harry S. Truman
Thirty-third US president (1884–1972)

LOVE UNMATCHED

When a mother and her baby share eye contact, something incredible happens – their heartbeats can synchronize!

This phenomenon is more than just biology; the simple act of gazing into each other's eyes strengthens the mother-child bond, fostering love and a sense of safety from the very beginning.

> In fact, she was both my first and second words: *Umma*, then Mom. I called to her in two languages. Even then, I must have known that no one would ever love me as much as she would.

Michelle Zauner
American singer-songwriter and author (b.1989)

LOVE UNMATCHED

> Children and mothers never truly part,
>
> Bound in the beating of each other's hearts.

Charlotte Gray
Canadian author (b.1948)

> **Being a full-time mother is one of the highest salaried jobs… since the payment is pure love.**

Mildred B. Vermont
American journalist, March 1954

LOVE UNMATCHED

> **"**
>
> Mama was my greatest teacher, a teacher of compassion, love and fearlessness. If love is sweet as a flower, then my mother is that sweet flower of love.
>
> **"**

Stevie Wonder
American-Ghanaian singer-songwriter (b.1950)

> Yes, Mother. I can see you are flawed. You have not hidden it. That is your greatest gift to me.

Alice Walker
American novelist and short story writer (b.1944)

Multi-Tasker, Magician, Miracle Worker

Ever seen a mum do 10 things at once and still look like she's holding it all together? Yes, it's basically magic!

From refereeing sibling wars to whipping up dinner (and snacks), mums are everyday miracle workers. This chapter shines a light on their amazing, multitasking superpowers.

MULTI-TASKER, MAGICIAN...

> **To describe my mother would be to write about a hurricane in its perfect power. Or the climbing, falling colours of a rainbow.**

Maya Angelou
American writer, poet and civil rights activist (1928–2014)

> Being a mother is an attitude, not a biological relation.

Robert A. Heinlein
American science-fiction writer and aeronautical engineer (1907–88)

MULTI-TASKER, MAGICIAN...

The record for the most children born to one mother belongs to a Russian woman called Valentina Vassilyeva.

Between 1725 and 1765, she gave birth to 69 children, including 16 pairs of twins, seven sets of triplets and four sets of quadruplets.

(Phew – that must have required some serious multitasking!)

> When you are a mother, you are never really alone in your thoughts. A mother always has to think twice, once for herself and once for her child.

Sophia Loren
Italian actress (b.1954)

MULTI-TASKER, MAGICIAN...

> A mother need only step into the shower to be instantly reassured she is indispensable to every member of her family.

Anon

> Twelve years later, the memories of those nights, of that sleep deprivation, still make me rock back and forth a little bit. You want to torture someone? Hand them an adorable baby they love who doesn't sleep.

Shonda Rhimes
American TV producer and screenwriter (b.1970)

MULTI-TASKER, MAGICIAN...

Did someone say sleep?

Honestly, that's for people without kids. SuperMums know that to survive 3am existential chats with a toddler, you need coffee, dry shampoo and sheer willpower.

In those early days, you forget what day it is, where your phone is – and sometimes, even your own name!

> Sleep, at this point, is just a concept, something I'm looking forward to investigating in the future.

Amy Poehler
American actress and comedian (b.1971)

MULTI-TASKER, MAGICIAN...

> **Meditation is my thing. But I'm not going to lie: sometimes, I go into my closet and lock the door so no one can find me.**

Gwen Stefani
American singer-songwriter and fashion designer (b.1969)

> God could not be everywhere, so he created mothers.

Jewish proverb

MULTI-TASKER, MAGICIAN...

Part 2:
SuperMum Movies

Erin Brockovich (2000) – Based on a true story, Julia Roberts plays a single mother who takes on a big corporation.

The Blind Side (2009) – Sandra Bullock plays Leigh Anne Tuohy, a determined mum who changes the life of a homeless teenager.

Little Miss Sunshine (2006) – Toni Collette plays an endlessly patient mum keeping her wonderfully weird family from totally unravelling.

Lion (2016) – Inspired by a real family, this is the tale of a loving adoptive mum who stands by her son as he searches for his birth family.

Terminator 2: Judgment Day (1991) - Linda Hamilton's Sarah Connor is the ultimate action-mum, fighting to protect her son and save the future.

Brave (2012) - Queen Elinor tries to tame her wild daughter Merida while dealing with a slight bear-related hiccup.

Everything Everywhere All at Once (2022) - A multiverse-hopping mother trying to save not just the universe, but her relationship with her daughter.

Freaky Friday (2003) - Jamie Lee Curtis swaps bodies with her teenage daughter and finds out just how hard high school really is.

MULTI-TASKER, MAGICIAN...

> **Motherhood is basically finding activities for children in three-hour pockets of time for the rest of your life.**

Mindy Kaling
American actress and comedian (b. 1979)

> Any mother could perform the jobs of several air traffic controllers with ease.

Lisa Alther
American author (b.1944)

MULTI-TASKER, MAGICIAN...

Studies show that during peak parenting times - typically mornings and early evenings - mothers often juggle more than 20 different tasks per hour.

From making breakfast and packing lunches to answering questions, calming meltdowns and remembering every appointment, it's a finely tuned balancing act.

> **If evolution really works, how come mothers only have two hands?**

Milton Berle
American actor and comedian (1908–2002)

MULTI-TASKER, MAGICIAN...

> **A toy Tamagotchi is more communicative than a human baby, OK? Because the toy will at least tell you when it poos.**

Ali Wong
American comedian and actress (b.1982)

> Silence is golden.
> Unless you have kids.
> Then silence is just suspicious.

Anon

MULTI-TASKER, MAGICIAN...

10 Songs

From heartfelt tributes to life lessons, these tracks honour the women who shape us in unforgettable ways.

Spice Girls - "Mama"
Appreciating mums and the unconditional love they give.

Boyz II Men - "A Song for Mama"
A soulful ballad celebrating the strength and sacrifice of a mother.

Taylor Swift - "The Best Day"
A gentle, nostalgic song about her close bond with her mum.

Christina Aguilera - "Oh Mother"
A powerful song about her mum's strength in leaving an abusive relationship.

SUPER MUM

Alicia Keys - "Speechless" (feat. Eve)
Written shortly after the birth of her son.

Pink - "Family Portrait"
Explores family dynamics, with Mum at the centre.

Backstreet Boys - "The Perfect Fan"
A touching tribute to a mother being a lifelong supporter.

Elvis Presley - "That's All Right, Mama"
This rockabilly classic showcases Elvis's early style and influence.

2Pac - "Dear Mama"
This iconic hip hop song is an emotional tribute.

The Shirelles - "Mama Said"
A classic pop tune about the life lessons passed on by mothers.

MULTI-TASKER, MAGICIAN...

> The fastest way to break the cycle of perfectionism and become a fearless mother is to give up the idea of doing it 'perfectly'. Indeed to embrace uncertainty and imperfection.

Arianna Huffington
Greek-American writer and businesswoman

> Personally, I've always known that I wanted to go back to work because I'm confident, and I'm certain that my daughter will have a better mother in me if I'm doing the things that I'm excited about and that I'm passionate about.

Lisa Ling
American journalist and TV personality (b.1973)

MULTI-TASKER, MAGICIAN...

In 2014, the card store American Greetings posted a fake job advert for a "Director of Operations" - requiring 24/7 availability, no breaks and no salary.

Interviewees were stunned - until it was revealed the role was actually being a mum. The video - called "World's Toughest Job" - went viral, celebrating the often invisible, non-stop work of motherhood.

Some of the job requirements were:

1. Must be able to work 135 hours a week.

2. Ability to work overnight, associate needs pending.

3. Willingness to forgo any breaks.

4. Work mostly standing up and/or bending down.

5. Must be able to lift up to 75 lbs (34 kg) on a regular basis.

6. PhD in psychology or real-life equivalent.

7. Unlimited patience.

8. Understanding of finance.

9. Understanding of medicine.

10. Valid driver's license, CPR certification and Red Cross membership.

MULTI-TASKER, MAGICIAN...

> **"**
> Parenting tip: maybe don't leave Hungry Hungry Hippos on the floor of a dark room.
> **"**

Rachel Dratch
American actress and comedian (b.1966)

> Motherhood: feeding them as a baby – and then through most of their twenties.

Anon

Across Place and Time

Motherhood is a global, timeless adventure. From ancient traditions to modern-day chaos, mums everywhere take part in the same wild and wonderful journey.

This chapter takes us on a trip through time and across cultures to explore how being a mum is both universal – and uniquely personal.

ACROSS PLACE AND TIME

> Children are the anchors that hold a mother to life.

Sophocles
Greek tragedian (c. 497–406 BCE)

> # Thou art my warrior;
> # I holp to frame thee.

Volumnia
Reminding her soldier son Coriolanus of her influence,
Shakespeare's *Coriolanus*, Act 3, Scene 2

Many cultures around the world have a "mother of the world" figure – goddesses who represent life, fertility and creation.

For example, Gaia in Greek mythology is the personification of Earth and the origin of all life. Similarly, Pachamama in the Andes is revered as the Earth Mother, responsible for fertility and the harvest.

The ancient Egyptian goddess Isis was seen as the perfect mother - loving, powerful and fiercely protective.

She was often depicted breastfeeding her son Horus, symbolizing divine motherhood and nurturing care.

ACROSS PLACE AND TIME

Viking mothers were no pushovers! While men in Norse society were often away fighting or trading, women managed the households and farms.

They had important legal rights uncommon in many other cultures at the time, including the right to divorce their husbands and inherit property.

> A mother's strength is the first shield a warrior knows.

Anon

ACROSS PLACE AND TIME

> "Let France have good mothers, and she will have good sons."

Napoleon Bonaparte
French emperor (1769–1821)

> If I have done anything in life worth attention, I feel sure that I inherited the disposition from my mother.

Booker T. Washington
American educator, author and orator (1856–1915)

ACROSS PLACE AND TIME

> **An ounce of mother is worth a pound of clergy.**
>
> Spanish proverb

There is but one and only one
whose love will fail you never.
One who lives from sun to sun
with constant fond endeavour.

Irish blessing

ACROSS PLACE AND TIME

> **Motherhood: All love begins and ends there.**

Robert Browning
English poet and playwright (1812–89)

> Mothers can forgive anything! Tell me all and be sure that I will never let you go, though the whole world should turn from you.

Louisa May Alcott
American novelist, short story writer and poet (1832–88)

ACROSS PLACE AND TIME

Mother's Day is one of the most celebrated holidays worldwide, observed in more than 100 countries – each with its own unique traditions.

From flowers and breakfasts in bed to heartfelt cards and public celebrations, Mother's Day is a global expression of love and gratitude for SuperMums everywhere.

In ancient Rome, wives and mothers were honoured with a special festival called Matronalia, held every year on March 1. This celebration involved giving gifts and performing ceremonies dedicated to Juno, the goddess of childbirth and marriage.

ACROSS PLACE AND TIME

Mother's Day Around the World...

US: Second Sunday in May. Created to honour mothers' sacrifices, inspired by Anna Jarvis in the early 1900s.

UK: Fourth Sunday of Lent (Mothering Sunday). Originally a day for people, particularly servants, to return home to their "mother church" and visit their parents.

Thailand: August 12. Celebrated on Queen Sirikit's birthday, recognizing her as the mother of the nation.

France: Last Sunday in May (or first Sunday in June if Pentecost falls on the last Sunday of May). *Fête des Mères* was officially established in 1950.

Egypt: March 21. Held on the spring equinox, symbolizing renewal and motherhood.

Argentina: Third Sunday in October. Originally tied to a Catholic feast and now a national holiday.

Indonesia: December 22. Commemorates the 1928 Women's Congress.

Ethiopia: During Antrosht festival (October/November). Celebrated at the end of the rainy season with singing and feasting.

ACROSS PLACE AND TIME

The clocks were striking midnight and the rooms were very still as a figure glided quietly from bed to bed, smoothing a coverlid here, settling a pillow there, and pausing to look long and tenderly at each unconscious face, to kiss each with lips that mutely blessed, and to pray the fervent prayers which only mothers utter.

Louisa May Alcott
American novelist, short story writer and poet (1832–88)

> The most beautiful word on the lips of mankind is the word 'Mother', and the most beautiful call is the call of 'My mother'. It is a word full of hope and love, a sweet and kind word coming from the depths of the heart.

Kahlil Gibran
Lebanese-American writer and poet (1883–1931)

ACROSS PLACE AND TIME

Five Global Traditions

These heartfelt customs celebrate life's milestones and strengthen family bonds:

Japan - Omiyamairi: A sacred newborn blessing at a Shinto shrine, where families pray for the baby's health and formally introduce them to their community.

India - Annaprashan: A Hindu ceremony marking a baby's first taste of rice - symbolizing the exciting transition from milk to solid food.

Kenya (Kikuyu) - Naming Ceremony: A vibrant community gathering where the child receives a meaningful name and blessings.

Mexico - La Cuarentena: A cherished 40-day postpartum rest, where mothers recover, bond with their newborns and are lovingly cared for by family.

Samoa - Fa'a Samoa: A warm tradition emphasizing the role of mothers and extended family in nurturing children with close community ties.

ACROSS PLACE AND TIME

> **The mother's heart is the child's schoolroom.**

Harriet Beecher Stowe
American author and abolitionist (1811–96)

> Mother is the name for God in the lips and hearts of little children.

William Makepeace Thackeray
English novelist and illustrator (1811–63)

ACROSS PLACE AND TIME

Classic Matriarchs

Discover mothers who shaped lives, challenged norms and left lasting legacies – in some of literature's most enduring family stories.

Pride and Prejudice by Jane Austen (1813) – Mrs Bennet is often portrayed as silly and socially anxious, but her driving force is a mother's desire to see her five daughters securely married.

Little Women by Louisa May Alcott (1868) – Marmee, the wise and loving matriarch of the March family, offers her daughters strength and moral guidance during the American Civil War.

The Mill on the Floss by George Eliot (1860) - Proud and socially ambitious Mrs Tulliver reflects the limited roles women could play in shaping their children's futures in Victorian England.

Wuthering Heights by Emily Brontë (1847) - Although maternal figures are largely absent, the second generation deals with the consequences of their mothers' choices.

The Tenant of Wildfell Hall by Anne Brontë (1848) - Brave Helen Graham defies social norms by leaving her abusive husband to protect her son - an early feminist portrayal of maternal strength.

ACROSS PLACE AND TIME

> " A chef's palate is born out of his childhood, and one thing all chefs have in common is a mother who can cook. "

Marco Pierre White
English chef and TV personality (b.1961)

> I don't know what it is about food your mother makes for you, especially when it's something that anyone can make – pancakes, meat loaf, tuna salad – but it carries a certain taste of memory.

Mitch Albom
American author and talk show host (b.1958)

ACROSS PLACE AND TIME

> A mother understands what a child does not say.

Jewish Proverb

> There is only one pretty child in the world, and every mother has it.

Chinese Proverb

ACROSS PLACE AND TIME

When it comes to maternal rights, Iceland ranks among the best countries in the world.

Mothers are entitled to generous paid maternity leave, while shared parental leave encourages fathers to actively participate in childcare. Excellent healthcare services also help mothers balance work and family life more easily.

> Over the years, I learned so much from mom. She taught me about the importance of home and history and family and tradition. She also taught me that aging need not mean narrowing the scope of your activities and interests or a diminution of the great pleasures to be had in the everyday.

Martha Stewart
American businesswoman, writer and TV personality (b.1941)

Raising Superheroes

Raising kids requires stamina and patience. There are tantrums, triumphs, tears and laughter – and *plenty* of sleepless nights.

This chapter is a tribute to all the mums who navigate the wild rollercoaster of parenting – the challenges, the victories and those unforgettable moments that make it all worthwhile.

> **I didn't fully wrap my head around the fact that there would be a person at the end of it. I read endlessly about pregnancy and what to eat and what not to eat. And then, I sort of prepared not at all for the actual baby.**

Ellie Kemper
American actress (b.1980)

> No one told me I would be coming home in diapers, too.

Chrissy Teigen
American model (b.1985)

RAISING SUPERHEROES

Magical Milestones

As a mum, you treasure countless unforgettable moments with your kids, from the earliest days of tiny fingers curling around your own to their growth into confident individuals.

Here are six to cherish...

The First Smile
That tiny, magical grin that lights up a mum's world and melts her heart instantly.

The First "Mama"
Pure joy in a word!

The First Step
Wobbly, adorable and often straight into Mum's arms.

The First Day of School
Backpack too big, shiny new shoes - and definitely a tear or two...

The First "I Love You"
No reminders, no bedtime script — just spontaneous love from your little human.

The First "Thanks, Mum" (without being asked)
Unprompted gratitude feels like the ultimate reward!

> Motherhood: Powered by love. Fuelled by coffee. Sustained by wine.

Anon

> **Biology is the least of what makes someone a mother.**

Oprah Winfrey
American host and TV producer (b.1954)

RAISING SUPERHEROES

> "
> A mother's life, you see, is one long succession of dramas, now soft and tender, now terrible. Not an hour but has its joys and fears.
> "

Honoré de Balzac
French novelist and playwright (1799–1850)

> Women know the way to rear up children (to be just). They know a simple, merry, tender knack of tying sashes, fitting baby-shoes, and stringing pretty words that make no sense. And kissing full sense into empty words.

Elizabeth Barrett Browning
English poet (1806–61)

> **What a mother sings to the cradle goes all the way down to the coffin.**

Henry Ward Beecher
American minister (1813–87)

> **Setting a good example for your children takes all the fun out of middle age.**

William Feather
American publisher and writer (1889–1981)

RAISING SUPERHEROES

Me Time

Being a SuperMum is *super* exhausting. These quick self-care tips will help you recharge and carve out some much-needed "me time" – because even superheroes deserve a well-earned break!

Secret Ninja Breaths
Sneak in 10 deep breaths when no one's watching – and recharge your superhero powers!

The "Hide and Sleep" Power Nap
Find a cozy spot, close your eyes for 20 minutes and pretend you're on a tropical island.

Snack Like a Queen
Treat yourself to that forbidden chocolate bar - because, yes, you totally earned it.

Dance Party for One
Blast your favourite song and shake off the stress like nobody's watching (except maybe the kids - and the cat).

The "Me-Time" Alarm
Set a reminder to disappear for five minutes — into the bathroom, a cupboard or anywhere with a lockable door.

Call For Backup
Phone a friend, partner or gullible relative and let them handle the chaos. No guilt allowed!

> When your children are teenagers, it's important to have a dog so that someone in the house is happy to see you.

Nora Ephron
American journalist and writer (1941–2012)

> You can learn many things from children. How much patience you have, for instance.

Franklin P. Jones
American journalist (1908–80)

RAISING SUPERHEROES

> **"**
> A mother is always the beginning. She is how things begin.
> **"**

Amy Tan
American author (b.1952)

> **"**
> Even as a small child,
> I understood that woman had
> secrets, and that some of these
> were only to be told to daughters.
> In this way we were bound
> together for eternity.
> **"**

Alice Hoffman
American novelist (b.1952)

RAISING SUPERHEROES

> The best way to keep children at home is to make the home atmosphere pleasant – and let the air out of the tires.

Dorothy Parker
American writer and poet (1893–1967)

> The quickest way for a parent to get a child's attention is to sit down and look comfortable.

Anon

Part 3:
You know you're a SuperMum when:

1. Your "me-time" is now a myth from a distant past.
2. You know that coffee is basically a food group.
3. You've worn the same outfit three days in a row.
4. You can answer "Why?" approximately 473 times before breakfast.
5. You've been asked "Are you tired?" more times than you can count – and the answer is *always* yes.

> Messy hair, don't care. I'm a SuperMum – not a supermodel!

Anon

RAISING SUPERHEROES

> "
> Like all parents, my husband and I just do the best we can, and hold our breath, and hope we've set aside enough money to pay for our kids' therapy.
> "

Michelle Pfeiffer
American actress and producer (b.1958)

> Waking your kids up for school the first day after a break is almost as much fun as birthing them was.

Jenny McCarthy
American actress and model (b.1972)

RAISING SUPERHEROES

> "A good mother loves fiercely but ultimately brings up her children to thrive without her. They must be the most important thing in her life, but if she is the most important thing in theirs, she has failed."

Erin Kelly
English writer (b.1976)

> **It just occurred to me that the majority of my diet is made up of food that my kid didn't finish...**

Carrie Underwood
American singer-songwriter (b.1983)

RAISING SUPERHEROES

10 Superhero Powers

From the little things that make a big difference to the simple acts that save the day, here are 10 everyday moments that prove mums have magic powers!

Magic Kisses – One kiss from Mum can heal scraped knees and calm fears instantly.

Bedtime Story Reader – Knowing exactly which story will make your child smile or sleep soundly.

Snack Summoner – Pulling a favourite snack out of nowhere, just when it's most needed.

Mess Detector – Spotting crumbs, spills or toys hidden in plain sight – it's all part of the job description.

Finding Lost Socks* - Somehow, mums always know where the missing sock is hidden.

Multi-tasking Magician - Cooking dinner, answering questions and doing laundry – without even breaking a sweat (well, the first bit is true...)

Soothing Voice - That calm tone can turn tantrums into giggles in seconds.

Superhuman Patience - Staying calm through endless questions and toddler antics.

Homework Helper - Turning confusing homework questions into "aha!" moments with patience and clear (well, you try!) explanations.

Emergency Cuddle Provider - Always knowing when a hug can fix everything.

RAISING SUPERHEROES

> **Usually, the triumph of my day is, you know, everybody making it to the potty.**

Julia Roberts
American actress (b.1967)

> My two-year-old referred to her coat pockets as 'snack holes' and this is what I shall forever call them.

Rebecca Caprara
American writer

Dear Mum...

This one's a big thank-you note to SuperMums everywhere – the queens of patience, creativity and endless love.

Mums, step-mums or mum-figures – this chapter celebrates all the ways they make life brighter, more fun and full of love.

> My mom has always been kind of my backbone. She keeps me strong. She is a mother, a friend. She is really everything to me.

Aerin Lauder
American businesswoman (b.1970)

> My mother... she is beautiful, softened at the edges and tempered with a spine of steel. I want to grow old and be like her.

Jodi Picoult
American writer (b.1966)

DEAR MUM...

> **My mother's beauty literally assailed me. Her smile widened her mouth beyond her cheeks, beyond her years, and seemingly through the walls to the street outside.**

Maya Angelou
American writer, poet and civil rights activist (1928–2014)

> I wish I could
> Shower your head with flowers
> And anoint your feet
> with my tears,
> For I know I have caused you
> So much heartache,
> frustration and despair –
> Throughout my youthful years...

Suzy Kassem
American writer and poet (b.1975)

DEAR MUM...

> A man loves his sweetheart the most, his wife the best, but his mother the longest.

Irish Proverb

> When your mother asks, 'Do you want a piece of advice?' it is a mere formality. It doesn't matter if you answer yes or no. You're going to get it anyway.

Erma Bombeck
American humorist (1927–96)

DEAR MUM...

According to a UK study, young children ask their mothers an average of 300 questions a day – or one every two-and-a-half minutes!

From "Why don't fish close their eyes?" to "Do you prefer the moon or the sun?", mums field a constant stream of curiosity, making them not just carers but explainers, negotiators and human encyclopaedias – all rolled into one.

> I cannot forget my mother. She is my bridge. When I needed to get across, she steadied herself long enough for me to run across safely.

Renita J. Weems
American author (b.1954)

DEAR MUM...

> Because I feel that, in the Heavens above,
>
> The angels, whispering to one another,
>
> Can find, among their burning terms of love,
>
> None so devotional as that of 'Mother'...

Edgar Allan Poe
American writer and poet (1809–49)

> If I were hanged on the highest hill,
>
> I know whose love would follow me still.

Rudyard Kipling
English journalist, novelist and poet (1865–1936)

DEAR MUM...

> The most remarkable thing about my mother is that for 30 years she served the family nothing but leftovers. The original meal has never been found.

Calvin Trillin
American journalist and humorist (b.1935)

> **My mother's menu consisted of two choices: take it or leave it.**

Buddy Hackett
American comedian (1924–2003)

DEAR MUM...

I Love You

Kids have sneaky ways of saying "I love you" - from surprise ninja hugs to unexpected teen texts with a meme. Here are five little actions that speak louder than words...

The Surprise Hug
Out of nowhere, they grab you like a tiny (or not-so-tiny) bear - instant heart-melter.

Hand in Hand
Especially when they need you to "walk slower" or "carry my stuff" — love disguised as a request!

A Shared Toy (or Playlist)
Toddlers hand over their prized teddy, teens send you their weirdest song. That's trust.

That Side-Eye Smile
The "I'm watching you but also love you" expression - subtle, and real!

Helping Out or Checking In
Randomly doing a chore or messaging "Sup, Mum?"- teen speak for "I actually care".

DEAR MUM...

> The love [has surprised me about motherhood]. Just the newness, the completeness, the wholesomeness of this love. It's just a different thing from anything I've ever experienced in my life.

Chimamanda Ngozi Adichie
Nigerian writer (b.1977)

> I'm much calmer now than I was before I had Annie. She had made me realize the truth of something that I'd heard all my life, but never really understood, which is what's important is the moment. Moment-to-moment living. And that life is right now. It's not tomorrow, it's not six months from now.

Glenn Close
American actress (b.1947)

DEAR MUM...

Mums in Books

Fictional SuperMums shape worlds with love, grit and power. Let's meet some matriarchs who prove that motherhood is the ultimate superpower.

Beloved by Toni Morrison (1987)
A haunting portrait of a mother's trauma, love and sacrifice in the aftermath of slavery.

The Joy Luck Club by Amy Tan (1989)
An emotional story about Chinese-American mothers and daughters navigating legacy and connection.

Room by Emma Donoghue (2010)
Showcases a mother's fierce protection and love for her son in unthinkable circumstances.

The Light Between Oceans
by M.L. Stedman (2012)
Revolves around a woman who yearns to nurture a child, highlighting the complexities of motherhood.

Everything I Never Told You
by Celeste Ng (2014)
A gripping family drama exploring motherhood through the lens of cultural and generational tension.

Big Little Lies by Liane Moriarty (2014)
Includes several mother characters who are deeply caring and protective of their children.

DEAR MUM...

> Your arms were always open
> when I needed a hug.
>
> Your heart understood
> when I needed a friend.
>
> Your gentle eyes were stern
> when I needed a lesson.
>
> Your strength and love has guided
> me and gave me wings to fly.

Sarah Malin
English writer (b.1968)

> My mother was a very wild Australian woman. When we were in Africa, she could kill a snake with one blow from a crow bar, which she kept at the back door.

Mem Fox
Australian writer (b.1946)

DEAR MUM...

A mother holds her children's hands for a while, but their hearts forever.

Anon

> One night when [Chelsea] was crying, as babies do, I said, 'You've never been a baby before and I've never been a mother. We're just going to have to work together and figure this out.' But it was the greatest experience of my life.

Hillary Clinton
Lawyer and former US Secretary of State (b.1947)

DEAR MUM...

> My mother is in the bones of my spine, keeping me straight and true. She is in my blood, making sure it runs rich and strong. She is in the beating of my heart. I cannot now imagine a life without her.

Kristin Hannah
American writer (b.1960)

SUPER MUM

> **"**
> A sweater is a garment worn by a child when the mother feels chilly.
> **"**

Barbara Johnson
American writer (1927–2007)

DEAR MUM...

> **There's no way to be a perfect mother, and a million ways to be a good one.**

Jill Churchill
American author (1943–2023)